The ARTS

CINEMA

Nigel Hunter

Wayland

The Arts

Architecture
Cinema
Dance
Design
Literature
Music
Painting and Sculpture
Photography
Theatre

Cover illustration: Publicity poster for the film epic
The Last Emperor, directed by Bertolucci and first
shown in 1987.

Series editor: Rosemary Ashley
Book editor: Susannah Foreman
Designer: David Armitage
Consultant: Graham Evans, Lecturer in Film, Photography
and Video, Polytechnic of Central London

First published in 1989 by
Wayland (Publishers) Limited
61 Western Road, Hove
East Sussex BN3 1JD, England

British Library Cataloguing in Publication Data
Hunter, Nigel
  Cinema. – (The Arts)
  1. Cinema films
  I. Title   II. Series
  791.43

  ISBN 1–85210–773–1

OR 2/93

Typeset by DP Press, Sevenoaks, England
Printed and bound in Italy

35527

Contents

1 'The Seventh Art'

Cinema is the whole world of film, from *Bambi* to *Rambo*; from *8½* to *Z*; from *The Battleship Potemkin* to *Attack of the Killer Tomatoes*. The range of films is immense, and every year there are more. Cinema is big business – until television became widespread, films were probably the most popular form of entertainment this century. Films form a large part of television output, too.

Some films can be categorized by type, or 'genre'. Horror movies, westerns and musicals are all familiar genres. You can probably think of several more. Other films are not so easy to categorize. They may be associated with a particular 'school' of film-making, such as Italian 'neo-realism' or the French 'New Wave'. They may deal with issues – social, personal or philosophical. Or they may be more individualistic: films directed by Charles Chaplin, Ingmar Bergman or Andrei Tarkovsky, for instance.

The importance of the director has been much debated. Every film needs a director, of course. (Fritz Lang compared his job to that of a ship's captain.) But many other people are equally indispensible. Actors may be the first to come to mind. Then perhaps the scriptwriter and the camera operator, or cinematographer. Sound technicians and lighting specialists also play a prominent role. . . But film is perhaps the most collaborative of all art forms – look at the credits of any film: the individual jobs are far too many to mention.

Left Gone with the Wind, *a turbulent romance set in the American Civil War, has proved to be one of the most popular films ever made in Hollywood. It was famous even before its release in 1939, with publicity generated by the search for a female star: surprisingly the role was eventually given to an English actress, Vivien Leigh. The film's length, 220 minutes, was for many years a record for a Hollywood production.*

Right *A spectacular scene from Steven Spielberg's* E.T. – The Extra-Terrestrial *(1982). Science fiction/fantasy has been one of the cinema's leading genres from its earliest days, making full use of the medium's capacity for illusion, and – as here – of the ingenuity of special effects departments.*

Inset *Director Steven Spielberg (right) organizing a close-up shot of his star, Harrison Ford (left), during the making of* Indiana Jones and the Temple of Doom *(1984).*

The director's job is to hold it all together – to guide each person's efforts towards the single goal of the finished film. Ideally he or she is present at every significant stage of a film in the making. If there is a personal 'stamp' on the film it will usually be the director's, and for this reason the director is often considered the 'author' of the film. Only the producer has greater authority. The producer finances the film: he or she 'holds the purse strings'. If a film looks as though it might lose money at the box-office, the producer may insist on changes to it.

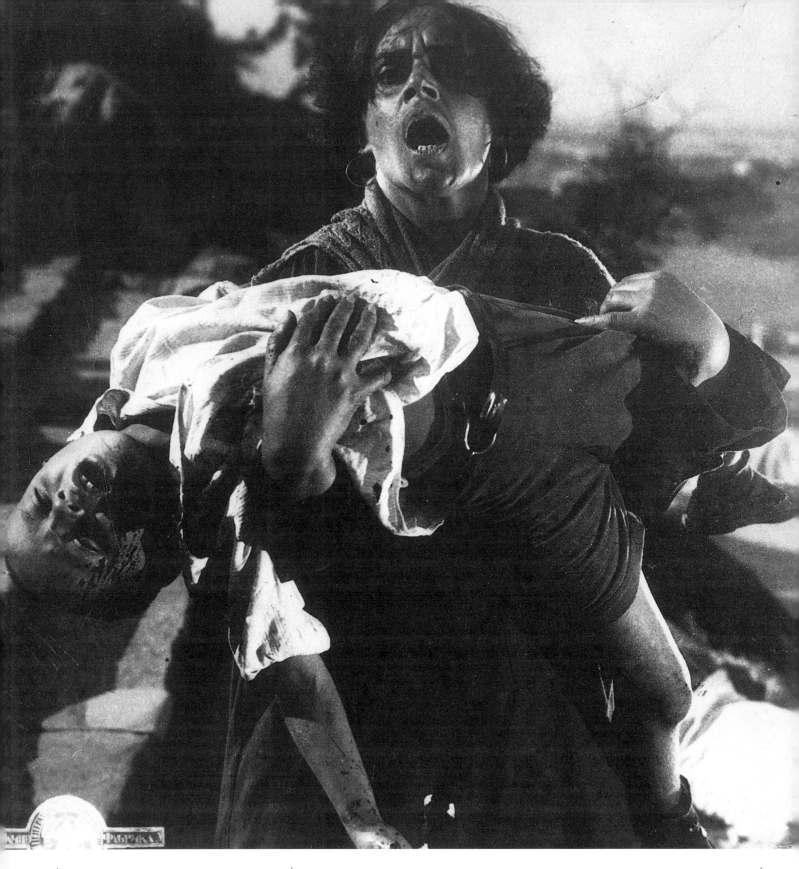

Over the course of a director's career, his or her main concerns as a film-maker will become increasingly clear. With the most original directors there will be a distinctive visual style – a consistent personal approach to all the possibilities offered by film. And similar themes will recur in succeeding films, even if the stories and settings are markedly different. The individual imprint of some directors can be quite unmistakeable. Anyone familiar with a few of Alfred Hitchcock's films, for example, would be likely to recognize another.

In mainstream commercial cinema, which includes all the popular genres, it is primarily action that matters – the events of the story: what happens, and what happens next. Ideally, the audience becomes so involved in the story that, for ninety minutes or so, they forget everything else. They may even be almost unaware of watching a film. For the director, part of the craft of ensuring the audience's emotional involvement may be to conceal the artifice that goes into making the film: to create and maintain an illusion of reality.

Commercial cinema aims to entertain, to reach a wide audience eager for thrills, laughter, romance, and so on. In this area of film production, the potential profitability of the film has much to do with whether or not it even gets made. 'Art movies', on the other hand, tend to be more thought-provoking, and less influenced by the profit motive. The action and events may be of less interest in themselves than for the way in which they are shaped by the film-maker. Often, the audience is well aware of the film *as a film*: part of the pleasure is in appreciating it as such.

In popular 'genre' films, similar kinds of characters often turn up again and again: the lone hero of the westerns, for example; the stage-struck lovers from so many musicals; or the crazed scientist from all those old horror films. Such characters are rarely developed in depth, and they 'grow' only minimally – if at all – in the course of the film. Their main function is simply to take their part in the story. Most people watching will be able to identify with one or other of the people on screen. This helps to keep the audience interested in the film.

Characterization in 'art movies' is likely to be deeper. The screen characters are generally less predictable than the stereotypes of popular cinema – more like real, individual human beings. Personal and social relationships receive more detailed treatment. But the distinction between 'film as art' and 'film as entertainment' is by no means completely clear-cut. Many films first enjoyed as straightforward entertainment (John Ford's *Stagecoach*, for example) later gain 'classic' status, receiving all the critical attention paid to any serious work of art.

This book presents a brief account of the development of cinema from its origins at the end of the last century. Compared with the classical arts – poetry, drama, dance, painting, music and sculpture – film is still a recent phenomenon. But its progress has been rapid. Films appeal to people of all ages and backgrounds, in every part of the world. As a cultural activity, cinema reflects and influences that world: at different times in different places it adopts a different character. Mostly, it entertains. Sometimes it informs, persuades and provokes. Occasionally it offers an aesthetic experience of the highest order. There is certainly a case for seeing cinema as the central art-form of our time.

Above *The lone hero of the western is a familiar figure to any film fan. Clint Eastwood – pictured here in* Pale Rider *(1985) – has starred in, and directed, many of the most compelling recent examples of the genre.*

Left *A shot from one of the most celebrated sequences in cinema history, the massacre on the Odessa steps in* The Battleship Potemkin *(USSR, 1925, directed by Sergei Eisenstein). A multitude of shots edited together in quick succession, the sequence is a prime example of Soviet montage (an isolated fragment such as this cannot convey the powerful impact created by the sequence as a whole).*

It is hard to imagine the impact of film in the mid 1890s. People were used to 'magic lanterns', which projected pictures on to a screen. They knew of devices like the 'Zoetrope', which gave an illusion of movement to pictures inside a cylinder. And they were familiar with photography, which captured the passing moment and fixed it forever. But a combination of all three, a moving photographic image, on screen? It was unheard of – until 1895.

In February of that year, in France, brothers Auguste and Louis Lumière registered an invention. It was a combination camera-printer-projector, which they called a 'Cinématographe'. During the rest of the year Louis was out filming. He made as many as a hundred films in this period, each lasting about one minute. Meanwhile, from time to time, the brothers demonstrated their invention to learned societies.

Simultaneously, in different countries, other people were working independently towards the very same end. The Lumières' device was matched in Britain by Robert Paul's 'Theatrograph'; in the USA by Thomas Edison and Thomas Armat's 'Vitascope'; and in Germany by Max and Emil Skladonowsky's 'Bioscop'. The Cinématographe was distinguished by being the first to be exhibited to a paying public. It also gave the new medium its name.

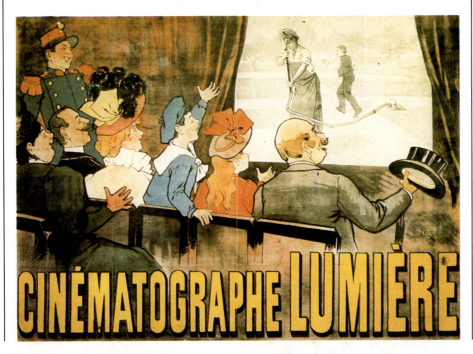

Left *One of several different posters designed for the first public film show, mounted by the Lumière brothers in Paris in 1895–6. The film on screen here is one of the most popular in the programme,* Watering the Gardener. *Notice that the audience is depicted much more clearly than the film – the message concerns a wholly new (exciting and pleasurable) experience.*

Late in December 1895 the first film poster went up: 'CINÉMATOGRAPHE LUMIÈRE'. In the opulent 'Indian salon' of the Grand Café in Paris the show was about to begin. It proved a sensation. By the following day, excited queues were forming in the street. For the price of a ticket, anyone could witness this newest marvel of the age. But few people guessed at its potential.

The Lumière programme consisted almost entirely of scenes from everyday life. Each film's content was neatly summarized in its title: for example, *Workers Leaving the Factory; Feeding the Baby; Demolition of a Wall; Blacksmith at Work; Boat Leaving the Port; Arrival of a Train at the Station.* The last film is said to have had the audience jumping out of their seats in panic; to inexperienced eyes, the express seemed to be heading straight into the room!

Only one film, *Watering the Gardener*, involved a situation set up especially for the camera. It showed a boy stepping on to a gardener's hose, then stepping off when the gardener checks the nozzle: of course, the man gets a faceful of water (and the boy gets thrashed!) Unwittingly, the piece gave an impression of how slapstick film comedy was to develop in the future.

Below *A cartoon from 1848 featuring a variation of the 'magic lantern', one of the many forerunners of cinema. Film itself, in its early days, was often considered to be little more than a fairground sideshow such as this.*

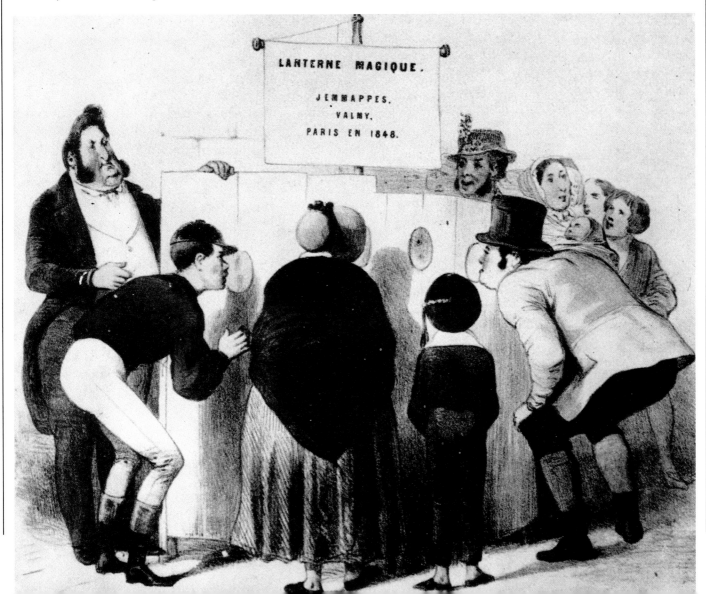

Above *A still from Edwin S. Porter's 1903 western,* The Great Train Robbery, *featuring the first cowboy star, 'Bronco Billy' Anderson. Although only eleven minutes long, the film was significant for its editing techniques and visually exciting outdoor scenes.*

Each of the Lumière films was composed of a single shot. The camera remained at a fixed distance from the action, and its angle stayed constant. The films were basically 'views' of places and events, and they were marketed as such. The brothers engaged other people to exhibit them around the country and abroad, and to add to the stock by filming new views during their travels.

One of the spectators at that first film-show in the Grand Café was a conjuror and theatre owner named Georges Méliès. He was so impressed with what he saw that he asked the Lumières to sell him a machine for his theatre. Politely, he was refused – and even advised that, while the invention could be exploited for some time as a scientific curiosity, its long-term commercial value was nil. Méliès was undeterred, however. He bought a projector from Robert Paul and constructed a camera to go with it.

As a professional magician Méliès was more interested in film's potential for trickery than in its ability to record real-life scenes. A half-minute film from Thomas Edison's company, *The Execution of Mary, Queen of Scots*, not only showed how a scene could be theatrically staged for the camera; it also showed how the medium could be manipulated for certain effects. During filming the camera had been stopped, just at the point where the actress's head was about to be lopped off. A dummy was put in her place, and everything lined up as before. The camera rolled once more, the fake head dropped into the basket, and the effect was complete. To the audience, the substitution was almost imperceptible.

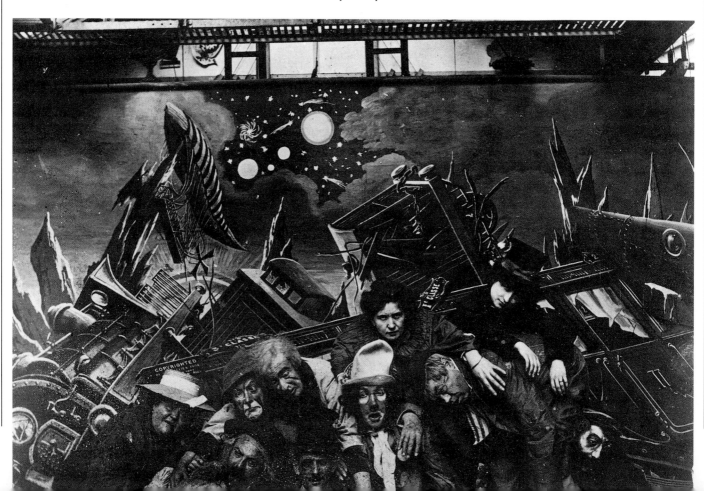

Méliès used similar means to create a whole range of effects. He made about a thousand films between 1896 and 1914, shooting them in his own purpose-built studio. He operated the camera, designed and constructed the sets, and often acted in the films himself. Significantly, most consisted of several scenes: some films extended to fifteen minutes in length.

Many were based on fairy-tales; others – such as *A Trip to the Moon* and *Conquest of the Pole* – resembled the stories of Jules Verne. Fantastic transformations were a regular feature: some achieved by stopping and starting the camera, others by the use of 'multiple exposure' (filming one shot over another). In various films, butterflies turned into bathing beauties; demons appeared and disappeared in puffs of smoke; a line of dancers emerged from a tiny box; a man's head swelled to enormous proportions; faces looked down from the sky like stars. Méliès even added colour to some of his films, by hand tinting the print.

He also re-staged various public events in his studio. One such was the coronation of Edward VII, with a waiter and chorus-dancer in the parts of King and Queen. Another was the notorious trial of Alfred Dreyfus – a *cause célèbre* of the day. Méliès' work brought him fame, but by 1914 his film-making career was over. By comparison with other people's work, his had come to seem old-fashioned. The camera's position remained the same throughout each scene, its viewpoint corresponding to that of a spectator at the theatre; and each scene appeared as one continuous shot. Elsewhere, film-makers (and audiences) had been discovering new possibilities.

In Britain, pioneer film-makers belonging to the 'school of Brighton' – such as G.A. Smith and Cecil Hepworth – made significant advances. They showed how scenes could be broken down into smaller units, and how sequences involving different points of view and different locations could be edited together to create a specifically 'filmic' form of narrative. No longer was film tied to the norms of theatrical space or time.

Edwin Porter, working for the Edison company, made similar progress. His film *The Great Train Robbery*, made in 1903, joined studio scenes with scenes shot out of doors; it cut from one set of characters – the outlaws making their getaway – to another – their victims being discovered – to another – the townsfolk enjoying a dance, then forming a posse to bring the outlaws to justice – to build an exciting, tightly-structured story. The film was to be a prototype for countless westerns to come. It also involved one of the earliest close-ups, featuring a bandit shooting straight at the camera (effectively, therefore, at the audience). This was not integrated into the action, however; it was shown separately, at the beginning or end of the film. Either way, its effect was startling.

With the work of D.W. Griffith, film advanced spectacularly. Between 1908 and 1913 Griffith directed almost 500 films for Edison's main rival, the Biograph company. The standard length was one reel,

Left *A photograph taken on the set of Georges Méliès' fantasy,* Impossible Voyage (1904). *Notice the theatrical backdrop suspended from a girder: this was the world's first purpose-built film studio. Unfortunately the photo gives little impression of the magical effects Méliès was able to create in his films – their sheer exuberance, however, is well conveyed.*

or ten to fifteen minutes. Their stories varied widely, though the plotting and characterization remained heavily influenced by Victorian melodrama. But in their formal design, and the understated, non-theatrical style of acting, the films were outstanding.

Griffith may not have been the first film-maker to use close-ups, longshots, fade-ins, fade-outs, iris-shots (shading around significant details), or a moving camera ('panning' from side to side, or 'tracking' forwards or backwards or alongside a subject); he may not have been the first to cut rapidly between various scenes and viewpoints; he may not have originated the use of 'atmospheric' lighting effects, or title-cards containing dialogue for the audience to read. But in his films, all these effects were combined for the first time to create a body of work with immensely strong dramatic and psychological impact.

In less than twenty years cinema had come a very long way. Throughout Europe and the USA the public was captivated, with millions queueing each week to see the industry's latest offerings. Silent cinema's 'golden era' was about to begin.

Below *The great American director David Wark Griffith (1874–1948), on set. The megaphone enabled silent-film directors to give instructions and guidance to actors while shots were actually in the process of being made. Griffith was widely admired, among other things, for the quality of the acting in his films. Under his direction extravagant theatrical-style gestures were replaced by a much more natural, restrained manner of movement and expression.*

3 Hollywood Silents – the Golden Era

During the First World War (1914–18), European film production was cut back drastically. Meanwhile, the American industry went from strength to strength. For some years it had been changing and growing – developing in ways that were to make American movies internationally dominant in the post-war period.

In 1908 the various rival companies, including Edison and Biograph, had banded together to secure a monopoly over the business. The group's policy was to make short films only – 'one-reelers', completed in just a few days. The films were shown in small theatres known as 'Nickelodeons'; the actors and actresses were not named. Movies were still considered a cheap form of entertainment.

The rise of new, independent companies provoked considerable hostility. The established companies – based mainly in New York – were not above hiring gangsters to wreck the efforts of these newcomers. Partly to distance themselves from trouble, and partly because of its natural suitability, some of the 'Independents' set up studios in California – in an outlying district of Los Angeles called Hollywood. There, among the orange groves, sage-brush and rattlesnakes, land was cheap, the sun shone all day, and there were plenty of scenic locations nearby.

Below *An interior scene being shot out-of-doors in the early days of Hollywood, while 'extras' (left) look on. Consistently good weather with long hours of sunlight was one of the factors that drew film companies to California.*

The new Hollywood companies encouraged public interest in their actors and actresses. With studio publicity, and the first 'fan magazines', the cult of the movie star began. There was also a move to much longer films. The success in the USA, in 1913, of two nine-reel Italian films – the historical epics *Quo Vadis* and *Cabiria* – proved that audiences were ready for lengthy, big-budget 'features'.

Two of the most spectacular came from D.W. Griffith, who joined one of the new independent studios. In 1914 he completed *Birth of a Nation*, a three-hour epic of the American Civil War and its aftermath. The film set intimate personal drama – the story of two particular families – against a background of momentous historical events. In technique and ambition it was far ahead of any film previously made: 'Like writing history with lightning,' President Wilson commented.

However, the film also brought charges of racism. Its heroes were the fanatical 'white supremacist' Ku Klux Klan, and its black characters (many played by white actors in make-up) were grossly stereotyped. In some cities there were protests and riots when the film was shown. Klan membership also increased considerably. Evidently, the movies were a cultural force to be reckoned with.

Griffith's next film, the monumental *Intolerance*, interweaved stories from four periods of history to illustrate its theme. It took fourteen months to make, and cost two million dollars – twenty times as much as *Birth of a Nation*. Eighteen thousand 'extras' were employed for crowd scenes; the sets for Ancient Babylon towered hundreds of metres into the air. Like its predecessor, *Intolerance* is now widely considered a masterpiece – but at the time, it was a commercial disaster. Griffith was never so extravagant again.

Right Inset *'The World's Sweetheart', Mary Pickford (1893–1979), in a studio publicity shot. First achieving stardom in some of D.W. Griffith's short films, made for Biograph, she subsequently became a co-founder of United Artists, and one of the richest women in the world. Her career faded with the coming of sound movies.*

Below *The clowning 'Keystone Cops', who featured in numerous slapstick 'shorts' produced by Mack Sennett between 1912 and 1920. The main event in each of their films was a long-drawn-out, hazardous chase through the streets of Hollywood. When the film crew arrived, ordinary business was suspended, and regular townsfolk kept well out of the way.*

Among the stars who emerged in this period, none were more popular than Mary Pickford, Douglas Fairbanks and Charlie Chaplin. Together with Griffith they formed a company, United Artists, in 1919. By then, the old-style East Coast companies had gone out of business. New, luxurious theatres, 'dream palaces', had replaced the Nickelodeons (in the most prestigious, full orchestras played the film's accompanying score). And the big stars were paid thousands of dollars per week.

Above *A scene from the Babylonian section of Griffith's* Intolerance *(1916). The gigantic sets and vast crowds helped to make this one of the most extravagant films ever produced in Hollywood. It was by far the most costly film of the era. By contrast, box-office takings were disastrously low.*

15

Mary Pickford was known as 'The World's Sweetheart'. In her most popular films, such as *The Poor Little Rich Girl* and *Rebecca of Sunnybrook Farm*, she played young girls. (Her innocent character contrasted sharply with the image projected by another star, the sexy 'vamp' Theda Bara.) The male 'idol' was Douglas Fairbanks, whose early films cast him as an ideal 'all American' type. Then, beginning with *The Mark of Zorro*, he became the archetypal 'swashbuckling' hero, performing spectacular acrobatic stunts with a winning, devil-may-care attitude. When he and Mary Pickford married in 1920, they were revered almost like royalty. Their mansion, 'Pickfair', became the social centre of Hollywood.

Charles Chaplin was 'Charlie the Tramp', with his twirling cane, his small bowler hat, his tight jacket, baggy trousers and big boots – a nimble, quick-witted survivor in a difficult world. Comic 'shorts' were a popular accompaniment to the big feature films. Many of the best came from Mack Sennett's famous Keystone Studios, where Chaplin had begun his film career in 1913. His unique talents quickly brought worldwide fame and personal power within the industry.

As well as appearing on screen, Chaplin devised and directed all but the earliest of his films. Increasingly, they showed his concern with social issues: short films like *The Immigrant, Easy Street* and *Shoulder Arms* contained pointed social satire. His first feature film, *The Kid*, drew inspiration from his impoverished childhood in the back streets of London. A characteristic blend of sharp comedy and soft sentiment, it was hugely successful with the public. But *The Gold Rush* remains possibly his best-known film. Many scenes are unforgettable – such as the one featuring Charlie's hut teetering over the edge of a cliff, while he and his partner scramble across each other to get out.

Harold Lloyd, another comic star, made such scenes his speciality. In high-risk dramas he scaled tall buildings, and wobbled on girders and ledges. Unlike Charlie, he usually 'got the girl' in the end. But among the other silent comedians whose films enlivened the twenties one was outstanding – Buster Keaton, the 'Great Stoneface' (whose expression never changed). Keaton's Civil War film, *The General*, was a masterpiece to rank beside Chaplin's best. For the authenticity of its period detail, it even bore comparison with *Birth of a Nation*.

To the film-going public, it was the stars who counted for most – and to the studios, star-worship meant money at the box-office. The presence of certain actors and actresses could almost guarantee a film's success. Among the most famous were the glamorous Gloria Swanson; the provocative '"It" Girl', Clara Bow; William S. Hart, the hero of countless cowboy films; and Rudolph Valentino, the seductive 'Latin lover', whose early death caused several suicides among his fans.

Directors were less well-known. Most Hollywood films followed tried-and-tested formulae; there was little room for originality. One name that could draw crowds, however, was that of Cecil B. DeMille. In 1914 he made the first feature-length western *The Squaw Man*. His

Right *Buster Keaton and* The General, *the locomotive in his Civil War comedy of the same name. Although for a long time neglected, Keaton is now widely regarded as a master of silent cinema. The delicacy and 'deadpan' qualities of his humour are often favoured over Chaplin's more frenzied and sentimental style.*

16

Left *Charlie Chaplin and partner (Mack Swain) in* The Gold Rush *(1925). Hunger and dejection are about to give way to panic, with the door swinging open to reveal a yawning chasm outside.*

patriotic wartime movies, like *The Little American*, and post-war comedies, such as *Male and Female*, caught the popular mood perfectly.

But DeMille's greatest commercial success was *The Ten Commandments* – a Biblical spectacular packed with sensational sex and violence. The censorship code instituted in 1922 permitted such scenes, as long as virtue triumphed in the end. For DeMille, it proved a profitable formula: 'Give me any couple of pages from the Bible,' he used to say, 'and I'll give you a picture.'

Erich von Stroheim was billed as 'The Man You Love to Hate'. On screen he was usually to be seen playing malevolent 'Prussian officer' types. But he was also a well-respected director. His films *Blind Husbands* and *Foolish Wives* took the subject of sex seriously, exploring character and motivation with subtle insight and great visual flair. The psychological realism was helped by the realism of the sets – complete and convincing down to the last detail – and by the effects of 'atmospheric' lighting.

Von Stroheim's characters, elegant or otherwise, are dominated by instincts of cruelty, lust and greed. *Greed* was the title of his most ambitious work – a ten-and-a-half hour film of Frank Norris's novel *McTeague*. The studio insisted on cuts, and eventually released the film in a two-and-a-half hour version which Von Stroheim disowned. Not only was the integrity of the film destroyed, so was the footage that had been cut. Nevertheless, there remain many scenes of compelling quality. The grotesque, pessimistic climax – two men, one dead, one dying, handcuffed together in the desert – was allowed to stand. Von Stroheim directed only a few more films. His uncompromising individuality found little favour in Hollywood: 'Art cinema' flourished mainly in Europe.

Left *A poster for one of Cecil B. DeMille's first sound films,* The Sign of the Cross *(1932). Like much of his work from the silent days onwards, it was a box-office hit, with a biblical theme and lavish amounts of sex and violence. In contrast to the poster, the film itself was in black and white.*

4 The European Scene

The 1920s was a period of revival and innovation in European cinema. The German industry was particularly strong, stemming from the formation of a national film unit, UFA, in 1917. Among UFA's first international hits were a number of historical 'costume dramas' directed by Ernst Lubitsch. In 1922, however, Lubitsch left Germany to begin a successful career in Hollywood. The most impressive German films of the period were very different from those of Lubitsch.

The Cabinet of Dr Caligari, made in 1919, set the tone for much of what followed in Germany. Directed by Robert Weine, it was a story of murder and madness, featuring a travelling showman-hypnotist and his zombie-like partner, Cesare. The sets were striking, dominated by unreal angles and painted-on shadows. The resulting claustrophobic, nightmarish effect is revealed to be entirely appropriate at the end: the film's supposed hero, who introduced the story, is himself mad – what we have been watching is his own paranoid delusion.

Below *A still from Robert Weine's Expressionist masterpiece* The Cabinet of Dr Caligari *(Germany, 1919). Notice the painted streaks of light and shade on the walls and floor, and the set's angular distortions.*

Left *Max Schreck as the vampire in F.W. Murnau's* Nosferatu *(Germany, 1922). This first cinematic treatment of the Dracula story conveyed a sense of genuine dread unmatched by later versions.*

Above *One of the crowd scenes from Fritz Lang's* Metropolis *(Germany, 1926). The film depicts a society of the future with strictly regimented workers and machines underground, and an élite class of the 'idle rich' above. Here the workers, led by Maria (Brigitte Helm), are staging their revolt. The vast city-scapes of* Metropolis *have influenced the designers of many subsequent 'futuristic' or science-fiction films.*

Paul Wegener's *The Golem*, Paul Leni's *Waxworks* and F.W. Murnau's *Nosferatu* were further examples of the German cinema's emphasis on morbidity and 'supernatural' horror. The sombre, ghoulish *Nosferatu* was the earliest film version of Bram Stoker's novel *Dracula* – and remains by far the most chilling. It was the culmination of what came to be known as the 'Expressionist' phase of German cinema.

The ability of film to suggest a character's state of mind was further explored in comparatively realistic productions. Murnau's *The Last Laugh* – the story of a hotel doorman and his mental disintegration, which follows upon losing his job – used lengthy, flowing camera movements in an attempt to convey its protaganist's psychological instability. Often we see the action from the doorman's point of view; the scene blurs, for example, and dissolves into distorted, fragmented images when he is under the influence of drink.

A more general impression of German society was given in the 'street films' of directors Karl Grune, Bruno Rahn, G.W. Pabst and others. Pabst's *The Joyless Street* was an outstanding example. It depicted Germany's contrasting worlds of wealth and poverty, decadence and decency, with unflinching realism. It was also notable for its editing techniques, in which 'cuts' were often made halfway through a moment of movement. Not only were the cuts less obvious than usual, they also propelled the narrative forward with added intensity. It was an important cinematic discovery.

Another director of note was Fritz Lang. His *Metropolis* was a futuristic fantasy in the Expressionist mould, a socio-political fable of oppression and revolt. Its stark geometric designs – sets, machines and humans *en masse* – made it visually one of the most arresting films of the decade, and also, perhaps, emotionally one of the 'coldest'. *M*, Lang's first sound film, was a psychological thriller based on a series of real-life child-murders. Sound is integral to its plot – a blind man identifies the culprit by the eerie tune he whistles.

With the rise of the Nazi Party in the 1930s, German cinema went into decline. Like others before and after him, Lang emigrated to Hollywood. In the USSR, meanwhile, cinema had been making advances in still other directions.

'Of all the arts,' said the Soviet leader Lenin, 'the cinema is the most important to us.' Film could communicate directly to everyone, regardless of their ability to read and write; it could be used to inform and persuade, and to spread the ideas of the workers' revolution of 1917 to the farthest corners of the USSR. Soviet film-makers were highly conscious of their political and cultural role.

The most significant advances came in the field of editing. V.I. Pudovkin, a leading director and film theorist, believed that editing was 'the foundation of film art'. Like many other major figures in Soviet cinema, he was a graduate of the Moscow Film School, where intensive study and experimentation took place. Griffith's *Intolerance* was analyzed with special fervour. 'Montage' is the term

Below *A frightening moment for Lillian Gish in* The Wind *(director, Victor Seastrom, USA, 1927) – the arrival of a would-be rapist. Seastrom was one of many well-known European directors who lived and worked for some time in Hollywood.*

applied to the resulting Soviet method. Its chief exponent was the director Sergei Eisenstein.

Eisenstein's films were built on the principle of 'contrast, conflict and collision'. Each shot – each image – was juxtaposed with others to give particular force and meaning. Cuts could be primarily intellectual in intent – like the 'metaphorical' cut from a group of workers being shot by police to cattle being slaughtered in the stockyard (*Strike*); they could serve an emotional purpose – increasing in tempo to build excitement, for example, or darkening in tone to suggest foreboding; or they could energize and intensify the narrative content – as in the short sequence of a sailor angrily smashing a plate in *The Battleship Potemkin*, assembled from eleven shots, each lasting a mere fraction of a second.

Potemkin included one of the most famous sequences in cinema history: the massacre of citizens by troops on the Odessa steps. By intercutting fragmentary shots of the mass, of smaller groups, of individuals in the crowd – of faces, hands, boots, rifles and other details; by combining footage from the top, bottom and sides of the steps, and by framing movement in alternating, opposed directions, the horror and confusion of the clash is powerfully conveyed. The faltering downward progress of a child's pram is just one crucial detail.

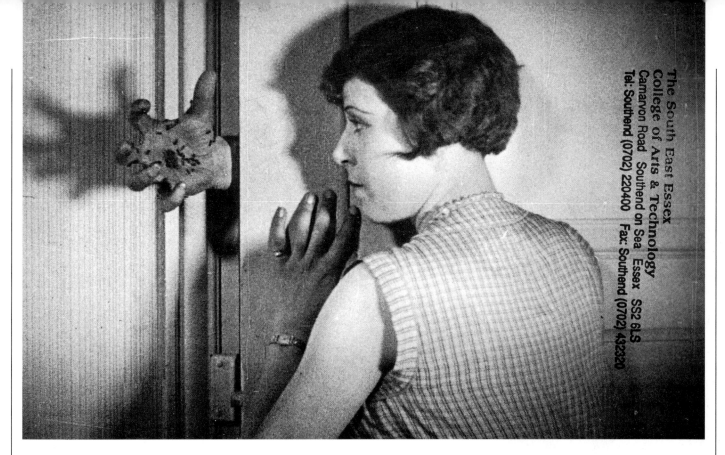

Above *This hand is crawling with ants: the image comes from Luis Buñuel's first film (co-director, Salvador Dali) the 17-minute surrealist jest,* Un Chien Andalou *(France, 1928). Over the next fifty years, in several different countries, Buñuel was to continue his career, working his various obsessions into some of the most bizarre, intelligent and fascinating films ever made.*

Left *Another image from the 'Odessa steps' sequence in* The Battleship Potemkin *(see also page 6). As a whole, the sequence lasts longer than did the real event in 1905. This helps to convey how it felt to be a victim during the event – at such times, time itself often seems to move more slowly than usual.*

Other noteworthy films include Eisenstein's *October* (concerning the dramatic events of 1917 in Russia); Pudovkin's *Mother* (dramatizing the revolutionary awakening of a middle-aged woman); and Alexander Dovzhenko's *Earth*, a poetic evocation of nature, people and machines. *The Man with the Movie Camera*, by Dziga Vertov, was a documentary of city life – also a celebration of cinema itself as a way of seeing.

However, when Stalin came to power, all these film-makers were accused of being excessively 'formalist', or abstract, in their approach. The great period of innovation in Soviet cinema was over.

Swedish cinema gained an international reputation, mainly through the work of two directors, Victor Sjöström (*The Outlaw and his Wife, The Phantom Carriage*) and Mauritz Stiller (*Erotikon, The Atonement of Gösta Berling*). Both were invited to Hollywood, but only Sjöström, renamed Seastrom, remained there. *The Wind* – a tempestuous melodrama of murder amid the harshness of nature – was perhaps the most outstanding achievement of his career.

In France, the American Surrealist artist Man Ray experimented with purely abstract films. *Return to Reason* was a torrent of images that deliberately made no 'sense' at all. 'Surrealism' in films reached its high point with a short film by Salvador Dali and Luis Buñuel, *Un Chien Andalou*. From the opening image of a woman's eye being slit by a razor, it proceeded ruthlessly to assault the audience with a succession of bizarre, dreamlike events. Abel Gance's spectacular *Napoléon*, and the mesmerizing *Passion of Joan of Arc*, by Carl Theodor Dreyer, were more conventional, and equally impressive. With such films, silent cinema reached its zenith.

23

5 American Talkies

'Wait a minute. . . Wait a minute. . .', says Al Jolson in *The Jazz Singer*, 'You ain't heard nothin' yet!' It was 1927: sound films – 'the talkies' - had arrived. The American public was wildly enthusiastic. All the Hollywood studios invested heavily in new equipment, and movie theatres throughout the country were converted for sound. Almost overnight, silent films disappeared from the screen. So too, for a while, did much of the visual sophistication of the silent years.

Since the soundtrack was recorded alongside the visual image, editing became difficult. Cameras had to be boxed – thus virtually immobilized – to prevent their operational noise being picked up by the microphone. Actors had to cluster together unnaturally, so the dialogue *would* be picked up (and the microphone had to be hidden – notice the strategically-placed flowerpots in so many primitive sound films!) For some Hollywood stars, the changeover to sound was disastrous. John Gilbert was its most famous victim. His high, squeaky voice went ill with his manly, romantic image.

Soon, however, the technical problems were overcome. It became possible to dub the soundtrack on after filming, and to mix several tracks together – dialogue, music and sound effects. More powerful directional microphones were developed. The 'boom' – essentially a microphone attached to a pole, held out of camera shot – allowed the actors to move around. Finally, a new lightweight casing, known as the 'blimp', did much to restore the camera's mobility.

Left *The Swedish actress Greta Garbo was one of the screen's most mesmerizing stars. Here, she is being directed by Clarence Brown in her first speaking role,* Anna Christie *(USA, 1930). Garbo's accent only added to the exotic charm of her screen presence, whereas some other stars were ruined by the coming of sound.*

Hollywood films continued to be dominated by the values of the studio system. Film was a commercial product, made on assembly-line principles. With certain exceptions, directors were assigned to a film only at the shooting stage; most took no part in shaping the story, or editing the filmed footage into its final form. And from 1934, all Hollywood movies were bound by a more rigid censorship code.

Each major studio was known for its own kind of films. MGM claimed to have 'more stars than there are in heaven'. Stars under contract to MGM included Greta Garbo, Joan Crawford and Judy Garland; Clark Gable, James Stewart and Spencer Tracy. Lavish family entertainment was the MGM style: *Mutiny on the Bounty, David Copperfield, Romeo and Juliet* and *Broadway Melody of 1940* were just a few of the studio's biggest hits. And in 1939 MGM released two of the most popular movies ever – *The Wizard of Oz*, and *Gone with the Wind* – both of which were made in the recently introduced process of Technicolor.

The next largest studio, Paramount, allowed its writers and directors more freedom. There was the inimitable Mae West, whose raunchy scripts and on-screen character ran foul of the censor; there was the misanthropic, gin-soaked buffoon, W.C. Fields; and, until they moved to MGM (where some say they lost their 'edge'), there were the Marx Brothers – lunatic clowns beyond compare.

Inset below *Dorothy (Judy Garland) and the Scarecrow (Ray Bolger) in a scene from the immensely popular musical fantasy* The Wizard of Oz *(1939; director, Victor Fleming). Until the 1950s, when competition with television made it commercially more viable, colour in films was usually reserved for the most prestigious productions.*

Below *The Marx Brothers, Harpo, Groucho and Chico, at the gates of the MGM studio lot in 1934. Out of work? Asleep? Or just kidding?*

For Paramount, Ernst Lubitsch made bright, sophisticated 'comedies of manners', such as *Trouble in Paradise* and *Ninotchka*. Josef von Sternberg was also widely admired for his stylish studies of erotic obsession and social decadence – most famously, *Shanghai Express*, *Blonde Venus* and *The Scarlet Empress*, all starring the sultry Marlene Dietrich. And Paramount also employed one of Hollywood's very few women directors, Dorothy Arzner, whose skilfully edited realistic dramas included *Nana*, *Merrily We Go to Hell* and *Dance Girl Dance*.

Fast-moving, tough-talking gangster films, such as *Public Enemy* and *The Roaring Twenties*, were a speciality of Warner Brothers. Warners also produced many 'bio-pics', including *The Story of Louis Pasteur* and *The Life of Emile Zola* – and the musicals of Busby Berkeley, with their extraordinary, kaleidoscopic dance routines. Musicals, of course, were to prove one of the cinema's most enduringly popular genres. Warners' *Gold Diggers* series and *Forty-Second Street*, with their 'let's put on a show' storylines, contained much of Berkeley's best work, including the 'Lullaby of Broadway' sequence in *Gold Diggers of 1935*. But the studio's best-remembered film may well be *Casablanca*, a superbly-crafted story of wartime romance and intrigue, with Humphrey Bogart in top form.

Below *After leaving the German UFA Studios, Ernst Lubitsch became one of the most successful Hollywood directors. Bluebeard's Eighth Wife (1938) was a typically witty comedy with a sexual theme, based on the well-known story of a man who murdered one wife after another.*

Right *Humphrey Bogart and Ingrid Bergman in a thoughtful moment from one of the most affectionately-regarded US movies of the 1940s,* Casablanca *(1942; director, Michael Curtiz). Bogart's performance as the owner of 'Rick's Café' extended his range beyond that of the gangster or private eye; he proved he could be a convincing 'romantic lead' as well. But the film's success stemmed from the contributions of many people, working together in close harmony.*

Below *The astonishing talents of Shirley Temple made her one of the USA's top box-office stars in the 1930s. Her career peaked when she was about eight years old – her age at the time of* Captain January *(1936).*

Above *The dance movies of Fred Astaire and Ginger Rogers provided audiences of the 1930s with much of the sparkle and glamour that the decade so conspicuously lacked.* Top Hat, Follow the Fleet *and* Swing Time *were among their most successful films. This poster advertises a film of 1949 which reunited them after a gap of ten years: it was to be their last film together.*

Twentieth Century-Fox concentrated on glossy historical and adventure films, and musicals with show business settings. Fox also produced the movies of Shirley Temple, the most precocious of all child stars – and one of the era's highest earners. The studio's most outstanding director was John Ford, responsible for such classics as *Young Mr Lincoln, Drums Along the Mohawk* and *The Grapes of Wrath.* In his westerns particularly, Ford emphasized the importance of landscape, as well as shared community values. His dominant theme was the bringing of civilization to the wilderness. History, in his films, becomes the stuff of myth.

Among the most popular films of RKO were the dance musicals of Fred Astaire and Ginger Rogers. During the economic Depression of the 1930s they were perfect 'escapist' films. RKO also produced the archetypal 'monster movie' in *King Kong* – a twentieth-century version of 'Beauty and the Beast', and an early triumph for special effects. *Citizen Kane*, the first film directed by Orson Welles, was a triumph of cinematic vision – a complex, searching 'biography' of a fictitious newspaper baron, daring in structure and technique alike.

Howard Hawks was rare among directors in working for several different studios. His films ranged across all the major genres, from gangster movies and 'action' pictures – like *Scarface* and *Only Angels Have Wings* – to sharply-scripted, fast-talking 'screwball comedies', such as *Twentieth Century*, *Bringing Up Baby* and *His Girl Friday*. All were among the best of their kind. Frank Capra, working for Columbia, made similarly witty – though more whimsical – comedies, usually angled towards the standpoint of 'the common man'. Among the best known were *Mr Deeds Goes to Town* and *You Can't Take It With You*.

Horror films, like *Frankenstein*, *Dracula*, *The Mummy*, *The Wolfman* and *Freaks*, were the special province of Universal. At their best, such films echoed the German Expressionist tradition of the 1920s in quality and character. A rather different form of fantasy was offered by Walt Disney – from his early Mickey Mouse cartoons, through the imaginative 'silly symphonies' series, to feature-length classics like *Snow White and the Seven Dwarfs*, *Pinocchio* and the spectacular *Fantasia*. In their use of sound and colour they were among the most adventurous of all movies. From the mid 1930s, naturalistic colour was another technical advance added to the range of options.

Monogram, Republic and other small studios concentrated on 'B-movies'. The B-feature became a regular part of the cinema programme, aiming to combat declining audience figures during the Depression years. B-movies were mainly cheap, low-grade westerns or gangster films; but for some directors, they provided a useful training in movie-making.

During the Second World War (1939–45), several major directors, including Capra and Ford, turned to documentary film-making for the government. It was sober, unglamorous work, but highly effective in boosting the US public's awareness of what was at stake. Fiction films also played their part. The character of 'the enemy'; the situation of occupied countries and embattled allies; the horror of combat; all were convincingly portrayed in many excellent films. Hollywood emerged from the war years with considerable credit.

Left *A frame from Walt Disney's first feature-length animation,* Snow White and the Seven Dwarfs *(1937). The quality of the drawing in the classic Disney cartoons has never been surpassed. Their appeal to successive generations of youngsters is maintained through regular, carefully timed re-releases.*

6 Europe: Towards a New Realism

In the years leading up to the Second World War, French cinema was at a peak of sophistication. British films also showed considerable flair and originality. But in the post-war period, it was Italian cinema which led the way. Hollywood was encountering strong competition.

Among the leading French directors of the 1930s were Jean Vigo, René Clair, Marcel Carné and Jean Renoir. Vigo died young, leaving just a handful of uniquely inspired films. Most remarkable, perhaps, was the short, lyrical *Zero for Conduct*. Beautiful and bizarre, infused with hostility and tenderness, the film depicted a group of schoolboys driven to joyful rebellion against their petty, mean-minded teachers.

Liberty was also the main theme of René Clair. His films were exuberantly fanciful comedies, packed with wild, inventive humour. Clair's imaginative mixing of music, sound and movement is especially admired. *Under the Roofs of Paris*, *The Million* and *Liberty is Ours* are widely acknowledged to be his masterpieces.

Above *A suitably menacing, suggestive poster for the atmospheric French police-thriller* Quai des Orfèvres *(1947), written and directed by Henri-Georges Clouzot.*

Left *Marcel Carné (left) directed several of the most widely-admired French films of the 1930s and '40s. Here he is working on a scene from* Three Rooms in Manhattan *(1965).*

Above *Alfred Hitchcock (centre) on the set of one of his first American films,* Suspicion *(1941). The film starred Cary Grant as a rich young man suspected of being a murderer.*

As the decade continued, the mood of many French films became more pessimistic. Marcel Carné's gloomy, fatalistic *Port of Shadows* and *Daybreak* both depicted a man helplessly drawn to his own destruction, anticipating the themes of post-war American *film noir* (see page 33). Equally sombre, though superficially very different, were *The Devil's Envoy* – based on a medieval legend – and *The Children of Paradise*, both made during the German wartime occupation of France. The latter, an evocation of nineteenth-century theatre life, offered a rich, complex portrayal of the relationship between art and reality. Many critics consider it the greatest of all French films.

Jean Renoir was one of the cinema's undisputed masters. His films were imbued with a harsh, even bitter, view of human character. In his work of the 1930s, society is shown to be in a state of terminal decay, its 'class' codes and conventions exhausted, capable only of destruction. Typically, Renoir's films revolve around a small, mixed group of characters in a restricted setting. *Grand Illusion* – set mainly in a First World War prison camp – and *The Rules of the Game* – set mainly in an aristocratic country house – were two of his finest achievements, rich both in ideas and in visual content.

British cinema in the pre-war period benefited greatly from the contribution of the Hungarian-born producer and director Alexander Korda. Korda's background included periods in the French and German film industries, as well as Hollywood. Of the films that he directed, *The Private Life of Henry VIII* and *Rembrandt* were outstanding. Of those he produced, *Things to Come* – with a script by H.G. Wells from his own book – was probably the most spectacular: exciting and uncannily prophetic, in scale and ambition it bore comparison with the very best of Hollywood.

Another highly admired British film-maker was Alfred Hitchcock. By the mid 1930s he had already made his reputation as a masterful director of suspense films – sly, artful thrillers that kept the audience on the edge of their seats. Frequent touches of humour made them all the more effective. *The Man Who Knew Too Much*, *The Thirty-Nine Steps* and *The Lady Vanishes* were three classics of the period. Hitchcock's career was to continue in Hollywood, consolidating his position as one of the cinema's greatest and most popular directors.

Social documentaries were another important aspect of the British industry. The term 'documentary' was even coined by the movement's leading light, the Scottish producer John Grierson. Basil Wright's *Song of Ceylon*, Harry Watt's *Night Mail* and Humphrey Jennings' wartime films *Listen to Britain* and *Fires Were Started* were compelling examples of what could be done in the genre.

One other documentary film-maker of the period also deserves mention – the Nazi propagandist Leni Riefenstahl. Despite their sinister ideological slant, her films of the grandiose Nuremberg rally of 1934 (*Triumph of the Will*) and of the Berlin Olympics of 1936 are indisputably powerful works. In their visual organization they achieved a rare – some might say 'pure' – filmic beauty.

For the Italian film industry, the end of the Second World War heralded a new beginning. 'Neo-realism' took fiction films out of the studio and into the streets. Real-life locations, non-professional actors and improvised dialogue gave the films an unprecedented degree of authenticity. Their stories dealt with the everyday lives of ordinary people in clearly defined social circumstances. There was little glamour, little romance and none of the escapism of Hollywood.

Among the major neo-realist films were *Rome, Open City*, made by Roberto Rossellini just after the Germans withdrew from the capital; Luchino Visconti's *The Earth Trembles*, concerning life in a Sicilian fishing village; and, most famously, Vittorio De Sica's *Bicycle Thieves*. This was the story of a father and son searching desperately for the man's stolen bicycle, without which he will lose his job. The film's poignant ending sees the man become a thief himself, caught and beaten by the townsfolk: only the boy (and the film's audience) knows what has brought him to such a miserable plight.

Neo-realism provided a grounding, or inspiration, for many other directors who went on to become leading figures in Italian cinema long after the movement's decline in the 1950s. These included Federico Fellini, Michelangelo Antonioni, Lina Wertmüller, Ermanno Olmi, Pier Paulo Pasolini and Bernardo Bertolucci. Individually, and as a whole, they have produced a rich and varied body of work which continues, in most cases, to the present day.

7 Widening Horizons

The post-war period was a difficult time for Hollywood. Legal restraints at home and abroad cut into the studios' profit margins, leading ultimately to a breakdown of the old-style studio 'system'. Many of the industry's most talented workers were 'blacklisted' (and some even imprisoned) during the notorious anti-Communist 'witchhunts' of the late 1940s and early 1950s; and there was a powerful new rival for film audiences in television.

One response to the first problem was a cycle of relatively low-budget features made in a neo-realist or semi-documentary style. These films usually concentrated on particular social problems such as racism (Clarence Brown's *Intruder in the Dust*), anti-Semitism (Edward Dmytryk's *Crossfire*), or alcoholism (Billy Wilder's *The Lost Weekend*). Certain crime films – like Jules Dassin's influential *Naked City*, shot on the streets of New York – were based on real-life cases.

In some quarters such films were considered to be 'anti-American'. Dassin himself was blacklisted a short time afterwards, and he left Hollywood to continue his career in France. (Another well-known director on the black list, Joseph Losey, became one of the most successful film-makers in Britain in the 1960s, with hits such as *The Servant* and *The Go-Between*.) One left-wing director who did continue to work in Hollywood throughout the 1950s was the German-born Douglas Sirk, whose apparently routine melodramas (*Magnificent Obsession* and *All That Heaven Allows*) are now considered by some critics to be veiled criticisms of American society during this period.

Left *Clarence Brown's* Intruder in the Dust *(1951) was a comparatively small-scale film which responded to pressing social problems with great integrity. It starred Juano Hernandez (centre) as a man unjustly accused of murder, and nearly lynched, by the racially prejudiced citizens of a southern US town.*

Above *Laurence Olivier's production of Shakespeare's* Henry V *was a major achievement of the British cinema in 1944, and possibly the finest example of 'Shakespeare on film'. Beginning in a mock-up of the Elizabethan Globe Theatre, the scene subtly expands to become filmically 'realistic'. Olivier not only took the leading role, he also directed the film. Its patriotic themes made it particularly relevant to Britain in wartime.*

One particularly successful kind of American movie of the 1940s and 1950s was termed by French critics *film noir*. Literally, this means 'black film' – black in two senses: visually (heavy shadows predominate); and in terms of mood, or moral tone. These films had few sympathetic characters, no clean-cut heroes or heroines, and no neat, happy endings. They portrayed modern society with cynical disgust, as sick and irredeemably corrupt. Crime, they suggested, was an inevitable, integral part of it. Wilder's *Double Indemnity*, Welles's *The Lady from Shanghai*, Hawks's *The Big Sleep* and Raoul Walsh's *White Heat* were just a few of the most outstanding examples.

The challenge posed by television brought about far-reaching changes in the American film industry. Many more movies were produced in colour (early television, of course, was black and white); cinema screens became much larger – the standard width increasing dramatically – and stereophonic sound was introduced. Film companies also experimented with '3-D' movies; but the range of effects was limited and the novelty soon wore off – the special viewing glasses needed to watch the film also caused headaches and eyestrain for some in the audience.

Above *Marilyn Monroe and Tom Ewell fall off a piano stool in Billy Wilder's sharp, mischievous comedy* The Seven Year Itch *(1955). Wilder and Monroe also worked together on the incomparable* Some Like It Hot *(1959). Two of the funniest Hollywood films of the 1950s, they both reflected the increasingly relaxed attitude towards sexual directness in the movies.*

Inset above Rebel without a Cause, *directed by Nicholas Ray in 1955, concerned the lifestyle of American 'teenagers' when the term was just coming into use. Its star, James Dean, died shortly before the film was released: almost immediately he became a legendary 'cult hero', as he remains to this day. The film was notable for its imaginative use of the new wide screen.*

With the new, bigger screen came many multi-million-dollar 'blockbusters'. *Around the World in Eighty Days, Ben-Hur* and *Lawrence of Arabia* were three of the most successful. Another was DeMille's re-make of his silent spectacular, *The Ten Commandments*. These made vast profits. Others, however – most famously, *Cleopatra* – were box-office disasters. The traditional genres continued, with many films of high quality: westerns such as *High Noon, Rio Bravo* and *The Magnificent Seven*; musicals such as *Singin' in the Rain, South Pacific* and *West Side Story*; thrillers such as *Vertigo, Rear Window* and *Psycho* (all made by Hitchcock); and comedies such as *Born Yesterday, Some Like It Hot* and *Pillow Talk*.

Science-fiction films and 'monster' movies also made a strong showing in the 1950s. Their doom-laden scenarios perhaps reflected contemporary unease with developments such as nuclear power. Some were excellent: *Forbidden Planet, Invasion of the Body Snatchers, The Incredible Shrinking Man, Them* and *The Fly*, for instance. Others – *The Blob, Teenage Zombies* or *Attack of the Fifty Foot Woman* – were quite beyond belief! The main audience for such films was the rising generation of teenagers, who were themselves being portrayed on screen, with considerable realism, in such movies as *The Wild One, Blackboard Jungle* and *Rebel Without a Cause*.

Japanese cinema first came to the attention of the West through the work of Akira Kurosawa, whose film *Rashomon* won the coveted Golden Lion award at the Venice Film Festival in 1951. *Rashomon* centres on a killing that takes place in a forest – but the event is seen in four different ways, each version being related by a different character: the concept of objective 'truth' or 'reality' is thus radically undermined. Subsequent films like *The Seven Samurai* (the basis of *The Magnificent Seven*) and *Throne of Blood*, a reworking of Shakespeare's *Macbeth*, confirmed Kurosawa as a director of world status – one still active today. His predecessors Kenji Mizoguchi and Yasujiro Ozu are now equally admired – the former particularly for his sympathetic portrayals of women in feudal Japan, the latter for his stylistically restrained, contemplative studies of middle-class family life.

The leading Indian film-maker Satyajit Ray began his career under the influence of the neo-realist school: *Pather Panchali*, his first film, used non-professionals in leading roles, and was shot on location in appropriate rural settings. Based on a classic Bengali novel, it focused on the life of a young boy, Apu. Before long, Ray completed two more films, covering Apu's growth to manhood and his experience of city life. Despite many later films of great merit, dealing with various aspects of Bengali society, the 'Apu trilogy' is still generally considered to be Ray's finest achievement. In the context of Indian cinema, its quiet realism made it almost unique, the vast majority of Indian films – then as now – being standard musical fantasies, primarily 'escapist' entertainment with very little cross-cultural appeal.

Below *A still from Akira Kurosawa's* The Seven Samurai *(Japan, 1954) – an epic tale of Samurai warriors defending peaceable villagers from persecution by bandits. Kurosawa's treatment of action and crowds, his editing, and 'framing' (as here), is often singled out for particular praise.*

Above *The American director Woody Allen, with Diane Keaton, in a scene from his wryly comic hit of 1977,* Annie Hall. *Many of his films pay homage to Bergman – usually in the form of affectionate parody. Few in his audience would fail to spot the poster here.*

Another director who came to international prominence in the 1950s was Sweden's Ingmar Bergman. *The Seventh Seal* and *Wild Strawberries* were probably his greatest films of this period. *The Seventh Seal*, a dark, poetic 'allegory' on the meaning of human existence, was set in the Middle Ages, with a knight playing chess against the ominous cloaked figure of Death. *Wild Strawberries* was equally profound in its story of an elderly professor reviewing his past as he travels through modern-day Sweden to receive an honorary university award. Bergman's cinematic probing into human consciousness and personality continued into the 1960s and beyond in a series of masterful, often very bleak, films which confirmed him as a director of rare power and originality.

Among the major French films of the post-war period were Jean Cocteau's stylish poetic fantasies, *Beauty and the Beast* and *Orphée*; Max Ophuls' ornate tales of sexual intrigue, *La Ronde* and *Lola Montès*; Robert Bresson's austere, intense *Diary of a Country Priest* and *A Man Escaped*; and Jacques Tati's hilarious *Mr Hulot's Holiday* and *My Uncle*. But it was the young 'New Wave' film-makers in France who created the greatest impression worldwide: their work amounted to a cinematic revolution.

Above *The French director François Truffaut (right) during the filming of* The Wild Child *(1969). The story, based on fact, concerned a child of the last century who had survived alone in a forest from infancy; who was discovered, and subsequently given a home by a sympathetic scholar (played in the film by Truffaut himself – hence his nineteenth-century costume, above). Like many of Truffaut's films, 'education' was the main theme of the film.*

Left *The chess game from Ingmar Bergman's masterly, atmospheric meditation on life and death,* The Seventh Seal *(Sweden, 1957). As long as the game lasts, the knight may live; he uses the time attempting to persuade Death that there is some meaning to human existence.*

François Truffaut, Jean-Luc Godard and Alain Resnais were three of the movement's leading figures. Truffaut and Godard were film critics and theorists – among those who had identified American *film noir*. Resnais' background was in documentary cinema. Each approached film specifically as a medium of personal expression: as an audio-visual *language* open to many kinds of manipulation. 1959 saw the release of their first features: Truffaut's *The 400 Blows*, loosely based on his own boyhood, concerned the life of a 'delinquent' youngster; Godard's *Breathless* was the story of a small-time gangster; Resnais' *Hiroshima Mon Amour* focused on the relationship of a French actress and a Japanese architect at the site of the first atomic bombing in Japan.

Among the stylistic effects common to these and many later New Wave films were abrupt 'jump cuts' from one episode or event to another, and within individual scenes; frequent use of unsteady, hand-held cameras; moments of fast or slow motion, and frozen motion; the inclusion of documentary and documentary-style material; and often, deliberate echoes and reflections of other films. By means of these and other techniques, audiences are kept constantly aware that they are watching a film – and that a film is not 'reality' but a conscious, artificial construction.

In Godard's later career – which has included much work on video – these strategies were turned to increasingly militant political purposes. Politics also came to the fore in the films of Constantine Costa-Gavras (*Z*) and Gillo Pontecorvo (*The Battle of Algiers*). Other important film-makers associated with the French New Wave include Claude Chabrol (*The Butcher*), Louis Malle (*Zazie in the Metro*), Jacques Rivette (*Céline and Julie Go Boating*), Eric Rohmer (*Claire's Knee*) and Agnès Varda (*One Sings, the Other Doesn't*). The stylistic influence of the movement on much of today's cinema (particularly in the USA) has been immense.

8 Contemporaries

The wide screen colour films of the 1960s were stylistically very different from earlier movies. Close-ups during dialogue scenes no longer needed to cut from one face to another – the wide screen allowed both speakers to appear at once. 'Long takes' with a fluent, moving camera were increasingly favoured over an assemblage of shorter shots (montage): this meant greater emphasis on the organization of elements within a shot (*'mise-en-scène'*). 'Deep focus' photography kept everything visually sharp, whether near or far from the camera; and 'telephoto', 'wide angle' and 'zoom' lenses rendered space in new, exciting ways. . . . Around the world, cinema was taking on new forms.

Post-war British films had been at their best in the work of David Lean (*Brief Encounter, Great Expectations*), Carol Reed (*Odd Man Out, The Third Man*), and Michael Powell (*A Matter of Life and Death, The Red Shoes*); and 'Ealing comedies', such as *The Lavender Hill Mob* and *Kind Hearts and Coronets*, were popular around the world. But the 1960s brought a new generation of film-makers. Many of them, and many of their successors in the 1970s and 1980s, were to move eventually to Hollywood, but meanwhile, British cinema was greatly enriched.

The early 1960s witnessed an impressive series of 'social-realist' dramas, often situated in northern working-class communities: Jack Clayton's *Room at the Top*, Karel Riesz's *Saturday Night and Sunday Morning* and John Schlesinger's *Billy Liar* were among the most memorable. Another, *This Sporting Life*, was the first feature by Lindsay Anderson, whose later work (*If. . . ., O Lucky Man, Britannia Hospital*) has amounted to a scathing cinematic assault on the British class system and its institutions.

Left *A scene from the Beatles' film, Help!, directed by Dick Lester in 1965. Made at the height of 'Beatlemania', this was an international showcase for the music and the carefully cultivated public personalities of the 'fab four'. Its visual zest was sufficient to overcome the demerits of a conspicuously implausible plot.*

Richard Lester's films with The Beatles, *A Hard Day's Night* and *Help!*, were quintessential 'sixties' movies, playfully exuberant in style and content alike. Ken Loach's *Poor Cow*, *Kes* and *Family Life* were entirely different in character, combining neo-realist and New Wave techniques to potent effect, in intimate portrayals of 'ordinary people' under social stress. Popular escapism was provided most notably in the long-running series of 'James Bond' spy-thrillers.

Beginning with *Women in Love*, the films of Ken Russell (who, like many contemporary directors, began his career in television) have been among the most admired, and controversial, of their time. They range from extravagant musical biographies such as *The Music Lovers*, *Mahler* and *Lisztomania* (not forgetting The Who's *Tommy*), to the more recent vivid horror-fantasies *Altered States* and *Gothic*. Another leading British director to emerge in the 1970s was Nicolas Roeg. Roeg's psychological fictions, from the early *Performance* and *Don't Look Now*, to such films of the 1980s as *Bad Timing*, *Insignificance* and *Track 29*, have consistently displayed a dazzling filmic imagination.

In the 1980s many more major talents have emerged. The 'Monty Python' group produced some of the best comic films of recent times in *Monty Python and the Holy Grail* and the scurrilous *Life of Brian*. Terry Gilliam's *Brazil* and *Time Bandits*, and Michael Palin's *A Private Function* (co-starring a pig) were more individual efforts. Other current directors of note include Bill Forsyth (the charming comedies *Gregory's Girl* and *Local Hero*); Neil Jordan (the fantastical *The Company of Wolves* and *High Spirits*); Derek Jarman (the highly individual *Jubilee*, *The Tempest* and *War Requiem*); Stephen Frears (the controversial social dramas of contemporary Britain *My Beautiful Laundrette* and *Sammy and Rosie Get Laid* – both written by Hanif Kureishi); and Terence Davies (the autobiographical Liverpool-based *Distant Voices, Still Lives*). Many of the most admired British films today are partly funded by television: an invaluable resource for younger film-makers, and for British cinema as a whole.

Above *With* Beverley Hills Cop, *Eddie Murphy became a top box-office star of the 1980s. Fast and furious action, combined with tough-edged, street-wise comedy, proved an irresistible draw. The film's sequel,* Beverley Hills Cop II, *was equally successful.*

This has to be the match of the day.

Gregory's Girl

GREGORY'S GIRL

Left *Bill Forsyth's gentle, observant comedy of growing up,* Gregory's Girl *(1980) was a surprise hit all around the world. It was one of the first of a large number of relatively low-budget British films which have heralded the arrival of many new talents in the industry.*

Right *Francis Ford Coppola's* Apocalypse Now *(1979) treated the Vietnam War as a large-scale 'psycho-drama', where virtually everyone is a casualty. The troops pictured here are renegade Americans, followers of the psychotic Colonel Kurtz. The plot concerns the efforts of a US intelligence officer to find and kill Kurtz. The film took so long to make that many referred to it during production as 'Apocalypse Later!'.*

Above *The interior of the orbiting space station in Stanley Kubrick's science-fiction spectacular* 2001: A Space Odyssey *(1968). Dealing with the evolution of humankind from 'the dawn of time' to the indefinite future, the film was a marvel of design and special effects. After twenty years, and many further developments in the field of science-fiction,* 2001 *still retains its original awesome grandeur.*

The influence of the French New Wave on American cinema became clear with the release of Arthur Penn's *Bonnie and Clyde*, the story of an outlaw couple in Depression America – a purposeful blend of humour, romance and graphically shocking violence. Like Sam Peckinpah's new-style rendition of the old West, *The Wild Bunch*, and like Dennis Hopper's hallucinatory bike-movie *Easy Rider*, its themes reflected the rebellious mood of American 'youth audiences' in the mid-to-late 1960s. Stanley Kubrick's *2001: A Space Odyssey* was oustanding in every respect: mysterious and fascinating in terms of its ideas, and in purely visual terms an enthralling, exciting experience for its audience.

Production in Hollywood was becoming increasingly independent of the big studios, which were by now largely involved in television production. Many stars and directors, such as Clint Eastwood – famous for 'spaghetti westerns' and tough police-thrillers – formed their own production companies. Directors as varied as Robert Altman (*M.A.S.H., Nashville*), Francis Ford Coppola (*The Godfather, Apocalypse Now*), Steven Spielberg (*Jaws, Close Encounters of the Third Kind*), Woody Allen (*Annie Hall, Manhattan, Radio Days*) and Martin Scorsese (*Taxi Driver, The Last Waltz, The Last Temptation of Christ*) became star names themselves, capable of attracting an audience in their own right. One major success among many low-budget independent films was Joan Micklin Silver's *Hester Street*, a story of turn-of-the-century immigrant life.

As before, one box-office smash could generate many like it. Popular genres of the 1970s included 'disaster' movies like *The Poseidon Adventure* and *The Towering Inferno*; spine-chilling supernatural horror films like *The Exorcist* and *Carrie*; epic science-fiction fantasies like *Star Wars* and *Superman*; and energetic dance movies like *Saturday Night Fever* and *Grease*. The 1980s have seen many films connected with the Vietnam War, ranging from the crass artificiality of *Rambo* to the agonizing realism of *Platoon*. With such films – and many, many more – the USA continues to enliven cinema throughout the world.

The West German film-makers Rainer Werner Fassbinder, Werner Hertzog and Wim Wenders emerged in the 1970s to great international acclaim. Of Fassbinder's forty-odd films, *Fear Eats the Soul, Fox and his Friends* and *Despair* were characteristic: all politically radical – fierce in their contempt for middle-class values – and humanly tender, drawing on the conventions of melodrama for emotional effect.

Right Flashdance *(1983), was one of several highly popular dance films of recent years. Like others, its success was tied to the quality of the music, with the soundtrack providing a hit single.*

Above *People waiting to enter a cinema in New Delhi, India. The Indian film industry is reputedly the largest in the world, with hundreds of movies produced every year, mostly in Bombay. Films from the subcontinent are also popular among the Asian communities of other countries. Some achieve even wider acclaim, such as Mira Nair's* Salaam Bombay *(1988), which has received high praise in many countries.*

Above right *A publicity shot for Werner Hertzog's massive undertaking,* Fitzcarraldo *(Germany, 1982). Hertzog's hero is determined to set up an opera house in the rainforest of Peru; but most of the effort in the film goes into manhandling this boat between two rivers separated by a steep slope. It was a lengthy, agonizing job, involving a local Amerindian tribe as extras.*

Hertzog's films – like *Aguirre, Wrath of God, The Enigma of Kaspar Hauser* and *Fitzcarraldo* – have a haunting, 'visionary' quality. Their characters tend to be obsessed by impossible schemes, or 'possessed' in various ways (in *Heart of Glass*, the whole cast acted under hypnosis). Wenders' films exhibit a fascination with American culture – music and movies especially. His characters are never 'at home' in the world: the world is seen as a wasteland – a desert of futility and isolation. Yet the films themselves are among the most pleasurable in recent cinema: from the early *Alice in the Cities* and *Kings of the Road*, to the 1980s *Paris, Texas* (made in the USA) and *Wings of Desire*.

Film-makers in Eastern Europe and the USSR were generally working under tight censorship controls: 'socialist realism' demanded straightforward narratives with an exemplary political theme. However, a short period of liberalization in Czechoslovakia in the mid 1960s opened the way for an exciting 'New Wave' in Czech cinema. Films by the feminist Vera Chytilová – *Something Else/Something Different* and *Daisies* – led the way. *Closely Observed Trains* (Jiri Menzel), *The Shop on Main Street* (Elmar Klos and Ján Kadár) and *The Fireman's Ball* (Milos Forman) were among the movement's most acclaimed films – mixing lightheartedness and seriousness, rendering their characters' inward feelings with exquisite skill. Forman has since become one of the most successful of Hollywood directors renowned for classics such as *One Flew Over the Cuckoo's Nest*.

Among Polish directors, Andrzej Wajda and Roman Polanski have proved oustanding. Wajda is best known for his early, harrowing wartrilogy *A Generation*, *Kanal* and *Ashes and Diamonds* – and for the more recent *Man of Marble* and *Man of Iron*, both infused with the spirit of 'Solidarity'. Polanski left Poland early in his career, the menacing, enigmatic *Knife in the Water* being his most notable early film. Subsequent British and American-made films, like *Repulsion*, *Rosemary's Baby*, *Chinatown* and *Tess* have been consistently compelling treatments of his major theme: the pervasiveness of evil in the world.

Some of the best Soviet films of the 1960s were literary adaptations – Sergei Bondarchuk's *War and Peace* and Grigori Kozintsev's *Hamlet* being two of the most highly-praised. A younger generation of film-makers included Larissa Shepitko (*Heat*, *Wings*), Sergei Paradzhanov (*The Colour of Pomegranites*), Ali Khamraev (*White, White Storks*) and Elem Klimov (*Agony*).

Andrei Tarkovsky's films have been admired throughout much of the world – but like other 'unorthodox' film-makers, he frequently encountered trouble having them shown in the USSR. *Andrei Rublev*, the story of a medieval religious icon-painter, was banned for several years. Then came the extraordinary science-fiction fantasy *Solaris*, often favourably compared to *2001*. Of his later films the autobiographical *Mirror*, charged with Christian symbolism, and *Stalker*, an allegorical journey through an industrial wasteland, were among the most expressive and widely admired. *Nostalgia*, his film of exile, was made in Italy; *The Sacrifice* was completed in Sweden shortly before his death. The present climate of change in the USSR can only benefit Soviet film culture.

Films made in South America, Africa and Asia have emerged in strength in the last two decades. They often serve explicit political and cultural ends, reminiscent of Soviet films of the 1920s. Tomás Alea's carefully-calculated comedy *Memories of Underdevelopment* and Humberto Solás's three-part historical epic *Lucia* are classics of revolutionary Cuban cinema – rich, subtle and complex.

Some South American films have involved considerable risks for their makers, the films themselves becoming acts of resistance against the regimes they document. *Hour of the Furnaces*, made in Argentina by Fernando Solanos and Octavio Getino, and Patricio Guzman's *Battle of Chile* were two such 'underground' films. *Veronico Cruz*, by Miguel Pereira – the story of a boy killed in the Falklands/Malvinas conflict – reflects the greater openness of Argentinian society today.

The thriving Algerian cinema has been led by militant film-makers such as Mohamed Lakhdar-Hamina, known for *The Wind of Aurés* and *Chronicle of the Years of Embers*. In Senegal, Ousmane Sembène has made witty, sophisticated films dealing with the cultural conflicts of emerging nationhood – among them, *Black Girl*, *Xala* and *Ceddo*. Solomon Lissé's *The Wind* and *Yeelen* are highly admired. Sarah Maldoror's account of the freedom struggle in Angola, *Sambizanga*, was widely acclaimed. African cinema promises much for the future.

Above *Isabelle Adjani, a leading French actress of the 1980s, in gorgeous finery for her role in* Subway, *(director Luc Besson, 1985).*

Above *Mel Gibson and Mark Lee, stars of Peter Weir's* Gallipoli *(1981) – a film based on the experience of Australian troops in a disastrous battle of the First World War. Weir's work was at the forefront of the 'New Wave' in Australian cinema which began in the 1970s. His other films include the haunting* Picnic At Hanging Rock *(1975), and* Witness *(made in 1985 after his move to Hollywood).*

Above right *The veteran British director David Lean, behind the camera, checking a scene during location shooting for his most recent film,* A Passage To India *(1985).*

Women film-makers are now emerging in greater numbers than ever before, reflecting long-overdue social changes. Most are explicitly concerned with feminist issues: Margarethe Von Trotta (*The German Sisters*), Helma Sander Brahms (*Germany Pale Mother*) and Doris Dörrie (*Me and Him*) in Germany; Chantal Akerman (*I You He She*) in Belgium and Diane Kurys (*Diabolo Menthe*) in France; in Australia, Gillian Reynolds (*My Beautiful Career*); in Canada, Patricia Rozema (*I have Heard the Mermaids Singing*); and in Britain, Sally Potter (*Gold-diggers*) and Zelda Barron (*Shag*)... to name but a few.

To appreciate films, of course, you really need to see them. Today, largely through television, films of the past and of other countries are more accessible than they have ever been. A short survey like this can only hope to offer a broad outline of the medium's history – of the thousands of films that constitute world cinema. The real education, and pleasure, is in the films themselves: clearly a major force in the culture of our century.

Towards a Film Career

For anybody considering a career in the movies, there are many hurdles to overcome. The competition is tough; you need not only talent and determination, but considerable luck as well. For those who 'make it', of course, the rewards are correspondingly great – though wealth and fame can by no means be guaranteed!

Those of you who feel you have an aptitude for film-making might make a start at school. The basic equipment you need may already be a part of your school resources; if not, you will need to mount a persuasive campaign, as even the simplest cameras and projectors can cost a considerable amount of money. Film stock is expensive too: to make just a five-minute film may involve a much greater financial outlay than you imagine at first, given the inevitable wastage caused by poor 'takes' and so on.

As a rule, the more detailed your planning, the less waste – of time and film stock – there is likely to be. Sketch out your film in advance, shot by shot, in the form of a 'story-board' (as most of the professionals do). In developing your talents over the course of several short films, you are likely to be repeating personally many of the discoveries made by the early pioneers of the medium – finding out what *works* filmically, and what does not.

Apart from the possibility of using school resources, or clubbing together with friends out of school, you may well be able to join an amateur film-making group in your local community. The experience of fellow-enthusiasts will be invaluable. Amateur film competitions, details of which are circulated to such groups, provide a spur to much work of high quality. Media resource centres also exist in many towns and cities – you can usually find their locations through libraries or local authority departments. Many such centres concentrate on video rather than film, however.

Despite the similarities in their end products, video and film require substantially different approaches and techniques. But the 'video revolution' of the last few years has opened up many exciting possibilities: you may find yourself drawn more strongly to the newer medium than to film itself. The convenience of 'instant playback' on a television screen of material you have just shot is only one of its obvious advantages. Another is the relative cheapness of videotape over film stock.

Specialist film schools in many countries exist to teach every aspect of the art (or business) to serious students; and many colleges and universities offer courses – involving both theory and practice – to degree level and beyond. The standard of entry to such courses is high, and places are restricted in numbers. To have some prior experience of film-making will certainly be helpful to any would-be film student. Most people who hope to enter the profession will be expected to have some such academic qualifications. Perhaps, in reading such a book as this, you are already on your way.

Further Reading

A few of the most accessible titles, of general interest, include:

Cinema by ANDREW HIGSON (Wayland Media Series, 1988)

A Discovery of Cinema by THOROLD DICKINSON (Oxford University Press, 1971)

Hollywood – The Pioneers by KEVIN BROWNLOW (Collins, 1979). Associated with the Channel 4 television series of the same name.

Movies of the Silent Years by ANN LLOYD (ed.) (Orbis, 1984) The same publishers have produced similar volumes on each decade up to the present day.

A Short History of the Movies by GERALD MAST (Oxford University Press, 1985)

Twentieth Century Cinema by BRENDA MANN (Wayland, 1989)

Interesting accounts of Hollywood include:

Adventures in the Screen Trade by WILLIAM GOLDMAN (Macdonald, 1984)

Hollywood by GARSON KANIN (Hart-Davis, MacGibbon, 1975)

One indispensable reference book is:

Filmgoer's Companion by LESLIE HALLIWELL (Granada, 1984 and Paladin paperbacks)

Some books specifically for young people on film techniques:

The Facts About a Feature Film by MARJORIE BILBOW (G. Whizzard/Andre Deutsch, 1978)

Films and Special Effects by SUSAN MEREDITH & PHIL MOTTRAM (Usborne, 1984)

Film and Video by TERRY STAPLES (Kingfisher, 1986)

Glossary

Aesthetic Concerned with the appreciation of the beautiful in art.

Cause célèbre A famous law-suit, trial or controversy.

Close-up A shot in which a small detail – usually somebody's face – fills the frame.

Deep focus A photographic technique that renders 'near' and 'distant' parts of a scene equally sharp.

Documentary A film of 'real life' rather than a fictional film.

Editing Preparing a film by re-arranging, selecting and rejecting previously filmed material.

Expressionist An artistic style that conveys strong emotions through deliberate distortions of 'everyday reality'. In cinema, relating particularly to certain German films of the 1920s.

Fade-in A photographic technique used to start a scene, in which the image gradually emerges from darkness.

Fade-out The reverse of 'fade-in' – the image gradually darkens until the screen is black.

Film noir A type of film that emphasizes 'dark passions' and violent crime, usually with an urban setting: applied particularly to certain American thrillers of the 1940s.

Frame One of a series of exposures from a strip of film.

Genre A term referring to films of a recognizable 'type', such as musicals, westerns, etc.

Jump cut A cut made in the course of an otherwise continuous shot, deliberately fragmenting the narrative flow.

Longshot A shot from some distance which includes the complete figures of its subjects, and often some background too.

Magic lantern A form of slide projector in use from the seventeenth century, usually featuring scenes painted on glass – a popular form of entertainment.

Mise-en-scène A term describing the arrangement of various aspects of a scene – sets, lighting, action, etc. – to be included within any particular shot.

Montage A term relating to editing – to the combination of shots in a sequence; in Soviet cinema of the 1920s, to the effects of certain kinds of cuts, and juxtapositions of shots.

Neo-realism Referring primarily to post-Second World War Italian films, with their use of non-professional actors and real-life locations, and their emphasis on social issues.

New Wave Referring primarily to French films of the late 1950s and 1960s – films forefronting various aspects of the medium itself.

Panning A side-to-side movement of the camera from a fixed point. From the word 'panorama'.

Realism An attempt to convey the 'reality' of life or society without imposing a personal view upon it (contrasting with 'Expressionism').

Slapstick Boisterous rowdy comedy.

Spaghetti western A cowboy film about the American West made in Europe, usually Italy.

Still A photograph of a scene from a film.

Telephoto A lens that magnifies distant scenes.

Tracking A shot made by a camera moving forwards or backwards on fixed rails.

Wide angle A lens that covers a broad angle of view, with some distortion of line.

Zoom A lens that can vary its focus over different distances, from 'wide angle' to 'telephoto'.

Acknowledgements

The author and publishers would like to thank the following for the use of their illustrations: Aquarius 27 (top); Chapel Studios 42 (left); Joel Finler 8, 43; Ronald Grant 18, 26 (inset), 27 (inset), 29 (inset), 31, 33; the Kobal Collection 6, 7, 9, 10 (both), 12, 13, 14, 15, 17 (both), 19, 20 (both), 22 (both), 23, 24, 25, (main picture) 26 (right), 29 (main picture), 30 (bottom), 32, 34 (main picture), 35, 36 (bottom), 37, 40 (right), 42 (right); National Film Archive 4, 5 (both), 25 (inset), 34 (inset), 36 (top), 38, 39 (both), 40 (left), 41, 44 (both); Topham Picture Library 28.

Index

Page numbers in **bold** type refer to illustrations.